Seven Advent Programs For Children

Doris Wells Miller

CSS Publishing Company, Inc., Lima, Ohio

Scripture quotations are from the *New Revised Standard Version of the Bible*, copyright 1989 by the Division of Christian Education of the National Council of the Churches of Christ in the USA. Used by permission.

For more information about CSS Publishing Company resources, visit our website at www.csspub.com or e-mail us at custserv@csspub.com or call (800) 241-4056.

ISBN 0-7880-1911-2   PRINTED IN U.S.A.

This book is dedicated to my former pastor, the Reverend Howard H. Bess, who kept telling me, "You can do it," and then allowed me room to create. Never did I hear a word of criticism and I knew that he would be there to help if I needed it. When I first joined this church, I was a shy, insecure young mother, but through the years he was able to draw from me insights and talent that I had no idea were there. It is my hope that I have been able, in some small way, to encourage the children in my care to find and express with confidence some of the talent in their possession.

Table Of Contents

Introduction

The most efficient yet enjoyable teaching tool available to the church school is drama. Both children and adults enjoy, learn, and respond in the process. In the past many public schools prepared an annual Christmas pageant which was enjoyed by children and parents alike, but with the laws as they are today we can no longer expect the public school system to take this responsibility. We, the church leadership, need to assume this role.

Seven Advent Programs For Children was written for use with pre-school through sixth grade. You are fortunate if you have a stage, but it is not a necessity. Our church is small with no stage and an unpredictable number of children, but we are fortunate to be able to arrange the sanctuary in any configuration. Props, sets, and costumes are kept simple. The most important ingredient is the support of the pastor and your church family.

Admittedly, there is a lot of work involved in planning any type of children's program, but with these easy-to-follow guidelines you will find that an enjoyable and valuable experience awaits everyone involved. Another benefit to the church is that it encourages the children to bring their friends to be a part of the experience. You will find that a special program will increase attendance in your church school and because these parents attend the production and bring their family and friends, you also introduce your church to the surrounding neighborhood.

I would be delighted to hear from anyone who plans to undertake this experience. Please feel free to write to me.

Doris Wells Miller
445 Stanford Place
Santa Barbara, CA 93111

Guidelines For Directors

1. **Program**
   a. Begin the process in September.
   b. Choose a committee and explore the reasons for presenting this program. Is it for church school growth, an educational event, celebration of the holidays, or just-because tradition? We have found a surprising number of neighbor children appear when there is a fun program.
   c. It is important to have the support of your teaching staff, church leaders, and the pastor.
   d. Clear the date and time for presentation with the church calendar. It should be a day that will not conflict with children "going to Grandma's for the holiday" or public school activities. This is not an easy decision. We hold our program the Sunday before the public school's winter break. In choosing a time, respect early bedtime for young children. It is possible to present it during the Sunday school hour or morning Worship Service, but we find it is best to use early Sunday evening, about 6 p.m.
   e. Consider the length of the production. These are young children and a program more than an hour long is more than they can handle.

2. **Selection**
   a. When you decide what program to present, you need to prepare the material. For a play you need twice as many scripts as you think. *(Scripts disappear.)*
   b. Count the number and ages of the children available. Are there children with special capabilities, talents, or needs?

3. **Planning**
   a. **Music:** Is there a children's or youth choir? Are there soloists? Selections noted in these dramas are only suggestions and are found in most church hymnals. If you have music that you prefer and that fits into the theme, by all means use it. Avoid presenting secular music.
   b. **Musicians:** Find a pianist or guitarist who will work with the children during their church school hour or, better yet, during the week. Give them a few months' advance notice.
   c. **Assistants: You cannot do everything yourself.** Enlist your teachers, friends, parents, or some in your church family. They will need to be at each rehearsal to help the children with their parts, plan and prepare sets, props, and lighting, and give feedback.
   d. **Rehearsals:** Plan the days and times, and clear this with your church calendar. A good time for **Dress Rehearsals** *(one is enough for young children)* is the day before presentation. This also gives time for last minute mending and ironing of costumes.
   e. **Party:** We follow our program with a family Christmas party where we invite the children, parents, families, and friends. We ask parents to bring a plate of "goodies" and the host, or our committee, provides punch and coffee. Ask a church member to host and let the person know he/she needs only to open his/her home and prepare a table to serve. Arrange for singing of Christmas carols and an accompanist. Our church uses this occasion to distribute Christmas thank-you gifts to the pastor and staff. This is not a necessity but a wonderful tradition to establish.
   f. **Recording Production:** Arrange for someone to photograph or videotape the program. A recording will be enjoyed for years and many parents may want to purchase copies.

4. **Rehearsal**

   a. In early November request from the church school superintendent, teacher, or responsible person permission to gather the grade school children in one place to "read" the program. If this is a large group, it may be done in two sessions. Let the children know that they will be participating in a special Christmas program. Read the entire script once; on second reading assign a different child to read each part. Then, after the start of each scene, assign another child to do the same. **You narrate** to give more control and direction. After the second reading, inform children of the first rehearsal date and that they will be assigned parts at that time.

   b. **Prepare two letters** to go home with children the day of the play reading: "**We Are Planning A Special Christmas Program** on December ___. Your child will have an important part in the production." Letters giving the date and time of the First Rehearsal go **only to the older children**. Two letters are necessary because you only want to work with the children doing speaking parts. The younger ones wait until the main characters are ready. Tell the "waiting" children that they will be needed (give a later date) so they will anticipate their being included. The letter should encourage parents to attend rehearsals and help out. You will be grateful for the extra hands.

   c. Write a child's name on each letter so that if he/she is not in church school that day, you can **mail** the letters to the child's home.

   d. Prepare a notice for your church bulletin, the same Sunday as letters go out, to announce the Christmas program with the date and time. Don't forget your church newsletter.

   e. It is my feeling that **every** child should be encouraged to be a part of all church school activities. Use them as angels and shepherds. Often a toddler will "steal the show" when he comes out in his angel costume with a tinsel halo hanging over one ear, or a mischievous child turns into a serious shepherd just by tagging along after the big kids. A child may act up at rehearsal but on the day of the performance, with parents and friends waiting for him/her, he/she usually comes through in an amazing way.

   f. If the younger ones who do not have speaking parts are included too soon in rehearsals, they become bored and disruptive. Invite them only to the Dress Rehearsal.

   g. Sometimes older boys do not want to be a part of a program. Offer them the opportunity to help with lighting, sets, or props. They can then be involved on their own terms and the program becomes truly a children's production.

   h. Those who attend the First Rehearsal are the ones most interested and should receive the best parts (unless someone who can't attend the first rehearsal but really wants to participate makes an effort to contact you). Be flexible; drama experience or talent are not necessary as parents will love whatever their child does. The child does not have to "look the part." You may be surprised at who wants to do what, and if the child feels strongly about it, you will have all his/her cooperation. The child will surprise you by the special meaning he/she gives to that part.

   i. After every rehearsal a letter goes home with the children. This letter re-states the date and time of the program, and rehearsal dates and times with the dates for the **Dress Rehearsal** in bold print so that parents will remember. As time goes on letters need to include more information regarding costumes, sets, and what you need from the parents. Mention the Christmas Party and invite them to bring "goodies" to share. Point out that they may bring family and friends to the production so there is time to invite others to share in this special Christmas experience. **Important**: be sure to give your phone number and request a call if their child will not be able to participate.

   j. Be sure to keep updates and reminders in the Sunday church bulletin and church newsletter.

5. **Doing The Job**

   a. **YOU are in charge.** Be gracious and considerate but do not hesitate to let everyone know what they should be doing. ***Without strong leadership nothing gets done.***

   b. At first rehearsal assign a leader to each group of children according to their parts. This group will work in the general area where their action takes place (such as shepherds in the field, angels in heaven). The leader assists the children with their parts and is responsible for bringing them in at the right time up through the presentation of the play.

   c. Each group and its leader is assigned seating at the back of the room. Here they will sit every rehearsal and on the night of the play. Familiarity brings security to nervous actors.

   d. Bring children together in a group following rehearsal. Point out all the good things you see happening. Discuss problems and answer questions about dates, costumes, props, etc. If requested they may take their scripts home to memorize; otherwise, collect them. Remind them of the next rehearsal date and time and distribute their letters as they leave.

   e. Hold a short meeting of your leaders following each rehearsal. Discuss their ideas and suggestions, and anything needing attention. Thank them for their help and tell them that you need them at all rehearsals. Let them know how important they are and remind them if they need to be away, they should see that someone takes their place.

   f. Assign two helpers to work on costumes (old ones refurbished, new ones to be made). Assign two helpers for props or sets that need to be constructed or repaired. **Do not do this yourself.** Invite parents, your women's or men's group, the custodian, a friend. The more people involved, the more interest and excitement is generated.

   g. At Dress Rehearsal, assign older children to be big brother or sister to very young children. This makes it unnecessary for adults to be running into the middle of the production to round up a stray child.

   h. Announce at the Dress Rehearsal that you want all the children and leaders to arrive, with costume in hand, an hour before the program.

   i. **Do not worry** when rehearsals become chaos ... they usually are. Join in the fun and laugh, then bring them together again by using your leaders and helpers.

6. **The Printed Program**

   a. Prepare a program and include the name of your pastor, church, address, phone number and the date and time. Also, the title of the program, author, children's names and roles, a listing of the musicians, production crew and all your leaders, with a thank-you to all who helped.

   b. Choose carols to sing, and use first verse only.

   c. **Keep it simple;** don't make the evening too complicated. There will be babies and other children attending and the place will be alive with activity and excitement.

   d. Invite everyone to the Christmas Party at the home of "use both names of hosts," their address and directions to their home. Do not put anything in the program about bringing "goodies." This information needed to be given previously in your letters home and bulletin announcements prior to the program. Guests feel awkward about coming if they think they should be bringing something.

7. **Presentation**
   a. Have Christmas carols playing as people enter. Is there a young person who plays an instrument? Ask him or her in plenty of time and let him/her select the music he/she wishes to play.
   b. If carols are to be sung, arrange for a song leader and an accompanist.
   c. Ask your Junior High youth to be ushers and, with two at each door, to pass out programs.
   d. In a separate room, before the program, gather around you the children who have parts. Take care that there are no distractions such as toys within their reach, or you will lose them. The children verbally go through the whole play until you and they are satisfied.
   e. Leaders will costume little ones as they arrive and then have them join older children in the circle. Leaders sit with the youngest around the perimeter of the circle so that they may keep better control. If a child becomes disruptive, it often helps calm him if an adult touches him lightly on the head or shoulder. They may temporarily remove an overexcited child.
   f. **Important:** Make sure that every child gets to go to the bathroom. Nothing is more embarrassing to everyone than to have to remove a squirming, uncomfortable child.
   g. Each group lines up with their leader. After straightening costumes, combing hair, wiping dirty faces (have they gone to the bathroom?), they may walk quietly into the sanctuary. This is peak excitement time. Reassure them that they will be great.
   h. Leader will walk his group into the room to sit in their assigned place until time to go on.
   i. You will take a bow with the children at the end of the program, dress appropriately. You need to be close to the front where the children can see you. Sit on the floor or on the front row in the middle. If you sit on the floor, sit on a soft blanket so that you may be comfortable and keep your clothes clean. Helpers sit at each end of the row (or on floor) with script to prompt.
   j. Speak to each child following the program, and say something nice about each one's performance.
   k. Attend the Christmas Party.

8. **Follow Up**
   a. You will find everyone will enjoy everything that happens because no matter who forgot their lines or made a wrong entrance, children are beautiful. When the children go on stage that Magical Night, dressed in their costumes, with music, spotlights, and their parents, relatives, and friends out front, they will do their best. You will feel the pride of every child and parent. It will be a good experience, I promise you.
   b. Write a thank-you note to each leader the following week. You will probably be asked to do this again next year and you will need the cooperation of every one of them.
   c. Give yourself a pat on the back; "You did a good job!"
   d. Please write to me and tell me all about your program. 445 Stanford Place, Santa Barbara, California 93111.

Step By Step Worksheet

for presentation of dramas and/or programs for elementary age church school children

Check off each item as it is completed

1. **Program:**
   a. begin process in September
   b. establish purpose
   c. enlist support
   d. clear with church calendar
   e. consider length of production

2. **Selection:**
   a. choose program, prepare material
   b. consider what children you have

3. **Planning:**
   a. music
   b. musicians
   c. assistants
   d. rehearsals
   e. party
   f. record production

4. **Rehearsal:**
   a. first reading
   b. prepare letters
   c. mailing letters
   d. church bulletin and newsletter
   e. use every child
   f. delay younger children
   g. involve reluctant older children
   h. First Rehearsal assign parts
   i. follow up letters
   j. updates and reminders in bulletin and newsletter

5. **Doing The Job:**
   a. YOU are in charge
   b. assign leaders to groups
   c. assign seating
   d. gather at end of each rehearsal
   e. leader meeting
   f. assign helpers to costumes, props, etc.
   g. Dress Rehearsal assign big brother and sister
   h. children to arrive hour before program
   i. handling chaos

6. **The Printed Program:**
   a. prepare program
   b. choose carols
   c. keep it simple
   d. invite to party

7. **Presentation:**
   a. music at beginning of program
   b. arrange for accompanist
   c. ushers
   d. gather children to do parts verbally
   e. leaders costume little ones
   f. bathroom time
   g. groups line up with leader
   h. children to program
   i. you sit in front row
   j. speak to each child following program
   k. go to party

8. **Follow Up:**
   a. you will be proud of the children
   b. write a thank-you to all your leaders
   c. you did very well
   d. write to me

Synopsis And Stage Directions
For Each Program

Blessed

You will need fifteen to twenty (or more) children from very young through the junior age department. The Primary children can be used as shepherds as their lines are very brief and can be memorized. You then can use any number of your youngest children as shepherds and angels. The music (familiar carols) may be sung by the children in the play, or a youth choir, or a soloist, or an instrumental.

The scene is set up in three areas. Center stage is the stable which can be a small chair for Mary and a manger for the baby. This area requires a spotlight that can be turned on and off. On one side of the stable there is a table with chairs around for the guests in the Inn. If it is possible, a simple doorway (take care this doorway is stable and will not tip over) could be placed between the table and the manger scene. On the other side of the stable (perhaps a bit to the side, yet where the audience can see them), a place for the shepherds to lie down in the fields. It would help if this area could be elevated in some way so that the shepherds can be seen. Sometimes the choir loft can be used with a piece of plywood over the top and a dark blanket spread out for the children to lie on. You will need to supply some type of step for them to get up to it. The announcing Angel can stand to the far side of the shepherds (perhaps on the step) with the little angels gathering around her/him where they can be seen.

The Play:

And Jesus said to them: "The kings of this world have power over their people, but this is not the way it is with you, rather, the greatest among you must be like the least, and the leader must be like the servant. Who is greater? The one who sits down, of course, but I am among you as one who serves."

The guests at the Inn were absorbed in their own pleasures and discomforts and the Innkeeper was busy with his guests. When the Holy Family arrived at the doorstep of his Inn, they were like any other travelers to him. No one could see beyond his own comforts except a young girl, overloaded with work and exhausted. She still found room in her heart to see that this couple before her needed help and took the time to find a place that was warm and safe. While everyone goes about his business, she, above all others, is the one who is blessed.

Jonathan's Cloak

Twelve children will be needed for the speaking parts. These may be from Primary age to Juniors. Any number of toddlers and very young children can be used as sheep. If they wander there is no problem with that; sheep wander. A flute (or guitar) played softly sets the feeling and plays in the background for the small child playing a flute on the set. A Youth Choir (or soloist) adds drama to the scene with familiar carols.

Center stage is set up with a few logs piled like a campfire (perhaps a small red light under the logs). Logs, rocks, or small chairs can be covered with a brown cloth to represent a campsite. Children carry botas or a cup to put water in from a large jar. Each carries his own food in a pack which could be fruit or small pieces of bread. A raised area to the side stage is needed for Jonathan and Daniel to meet with Joseph and Mary on their way to Bethlehem. A simple stable scene with a chair for Mary and a manger for the baby should be prepared on the other side of the campfire set-up.

The Play:

Before the Bible, as we know it, was written, stories of the Israelites' history and their relationship to God were told by the elders of the tribe. These stories were retold from father to son. The Shepherds in the fields with their sheep carried on this tradition by looking to the eldest in the group to tell the age-old stories.

The story of the coming of a Messiah is told and hope is renewed. Meanwhile, Jonathan, the son of the eldest Shepherd, has given his cloak to a young woman traveling the road to Bethlehem who was with child. When the Angel of the Lord announces to the Shepherds that the birth of the Messiah has taken place, they hurry into town to find the babe. There, covering the Christ, is Jonathan's cloak. Recall that as a man Jesus says, "When you clothe even the least of these, you are doing it for me." Without knowing with whom he shared his cloak, Jonathan had given it to the Christ Child.

Proclamation

A comfortable chair sits on the side of your stage for the "storyteller." A large Bible is placed on a small table or stand nearby out of which he will read the scripture.

This production has been written for older children, probably 8 to 12 years old. It is designed to provide an opportunity for your children to study in depth the Christmas story. Each child is to research a character that was involved in the Nativity. A storyteller relates the story from a large Bible, then introduces each participant.

Dressed as the person he is portraying, Mary, Joseph, Isaiah, King Herod, or a Shepherd, each enters and tells the congregation about the person he or she is portraying. This lesson needs to begin early in the fall so that the teachers may help each do the necessary research so that he or she can bring his/her character to life in an interesting way. Following his or her talk, each takes his or her place in the manger scene. After all have spoken, the stage then becomes the Nativity scene.

The Big Picture

Like the rendering of an old masterpiece of the Nativity by a famous artist, we see each person in the Christmas story come alive and tell you his version of what happened that special night when Christ was born, and then he will take his place in the scene. When all have finally entered the Nativity scene, they come together to freeze in order to form a portrait. People in the audience may then come forward and take pictures of the "masterpiece." It is not necessary, but it helps if you can build a large frame in which to hold this portrait.

The Play:

Dressed in the clothing of the person he represents, the child enters and walks to the front of the congregation. He tells us who he represents and what happened on that special night when Christ was born. Like a rendering in an old masterpiece of the Nativity by a famous artist, we see each person in the Christmas story come alive as the children come together to form a living portrait illustrating "the manger scene." The story purposely places the soldier and the Innkeeper to the side so that it becomes obvious to the congregation that they have closed themselves off from the wondrous birth of the Savior. As they chat, they will have missed the whole event. Come, see and hear what happened from the perspective of the person who could have been there.

The Christmas Story

Two chairs (you could use rocking chairs) for Father and Mother are set to the side of the manger scene. Father holds a large Bible. They invite all the children in the audience to come forward and sit around them as they retell the Christmas story.

The Play:

This is a good program for a small church with very young children and it requires minimum rehearsal time. It is Christmas evening. Mother and Father gather their children around them to retell the Christmas story. Many of the children are dressed as one of the participants in the manger scene. As the story is read, the children, one by one, take their place in the Nativity scene. When all the children have taken their places, Mother completes the scripture. The story ends when the manger scene is complete, and at that time it becomes a photo opportunity.

The Shawl

There are at least twelve children with speaking parts. You may use younger children as Shepherds (who arrive at the door). You could use a Youth Choir or have the children themselves sing (from their places) the simple carols that are indicated.

The scene takes place in three areas: Stage left is the Shepherd's home. Lydia (Mother) is at the table cutting bread and cheese and placing them in a small cloth bag. Tabitha is working at a small loom. Amos (Father) enters carrying a knapsack. Center stage is a stable. A crude divider stands near the back which screens what is the goat stall behind it. A small manger (with a short stool) sits at the front to indicate a stable. Stage right is the Inn door. Outside the Inn door is a small low table on which are stacked pots and pans and bowls which Jotham and Jacob are washing.

The Play:

Tabitha, who is spoken of so lovingly by her neighbors, in Acts 9:36-43, was not always such a generous, loving person. As a young girl she was rather vain and self-centered, but changed her life dramatically after an encounter with the Christ.

When she discovers the Christ Child sleeping in the humble stable, cold and helpless, she offers him her most prized possession in order to warm him. Her heart is strangely changed. Her view of life is enlarged and she no longer thinks only of herself as she realizes what she can do to help the suffering of others.

You Are There
Script to be used with slides and Children's Choir

This is a good presentation to use with a small group or for very young children, as it does not require a lot of rehearsal time. Costume your children and take them on "location" to take slides of them portraying various situations from the scripture. You may use a zoo, a farm, or animals in your humane society yard (if they have sheep or goats or horses), or any other natural type setting for the traditional Advent scenes. The background is not as important as the children are.

The Play:

When presenting the program, the older children read the scripture passages (preferably out of a large Bible) followed by your children singing carols. As each scripture has been read and the children have sung their carol, the slides are shown. One of the nice things about this presentation is that the children can watch themselves as they participate in the program. Then, too, you have a beautiful record to keep. Many parents may want prints of the slides that picture their children.

Blessed

The guests at the Inn were concerned with their own affairs, both pleasures and discomforts. The keeper of the Inn was busy with his guests. When the Holy Family arrived at the doorstep of the Inn, the occupants could not see beyond their own needs. But, a young girl, overloaded with work and exhausted, still found room in her heart to see the need of others. She considered their need and found a place where they could stay. While everyone else went about his own business and was interested only in himself, she above all others was the one who was blessed.

At times we are so full of our own need we cannot see the sufferings around us. We are encouraged by this child's example to notice how we can be of help. What blessings await us, for as the scriptures say, *"Truly I tell you, just as you did it to one of the least of these who are members of my family, you did it to me"* (Matthew 25:40).

Characters

Narrator	Ahab
First Man	Sarah
First Woman	Joseph
Second Man	Mary
Second Woman	Master
Nathan	Joram
Angel	

(Setting: A table with people gathered around to represent the Inn.)

First Man: Girl, girl ... bring us more bread.

First Woman: She is so slow ... you'd think she could move a little faster.

Second Man: I sure am hungry after the long trip with the caravan ... we must have traveled twenty miles today.

(Action: A young girl wearing an oversized apron enters, carrying a large tray of bread and wine.)

Second Woman: I'm certainly glad we arrived early this afternoon — hear tell that all of the Inns in Bethlehem are full.

First Man: I get angry every time I think about how we had to come to this godforsaken village just because our great-grandfathers were born here.

Second Man: Curse Augustus ... I'm losing money being away from my trade, just to be registered so we can pay taxes to that *tyrant*!

First Woman: All those poor, wretched people that we passed on our way into town ... having to walk all the way on that dusty road. They looked ... so ... tired and ... dirty.

(Action: Young girl serves bread to each as the people go on talking quietly.)

Sarah: Is there anything else that you wish?

First Man: Yes, pour us more wine ... and be quick about it.

(Action: There is a knock at the door. The serving girl sets the wine jug on the table and goes to answer it. A man and woman are standing outside. They look chilled and very tired. The woman is pregnant.)

Sarah: Greetings, friends, and what do you wish?

Joseph: We would like a room, please.

Sarah: Oh, do come in out of the cold.

(Action: The man and woman step inside the door.)

Sarah: Master ... master. Please come here.

Master: *(Pushes Sarah aside and speaks gruffly to Joseph)* Yes, and what do you want?

Joseph: A room, sir, for my wife and myself.

Master: There is no more room ... we are full. Go elsewhere. *(Waves his hand)*

Joseph: Oh, kind sir, please tell us where we may go? There are no more rooms in town.

Master: That is not my worry. I told you ... we are *full*.

Joseph: Dear, kind man, my wife is near to bearing her child. We can go no further.

(Master frowns, shakes head no.)

Sarah: Master, they are so tired. There is room out back in the stable. The straw is warm and it is shelter from the cold.

(Master gives Sarah an angry look.)

Sarah: But, Master, she is going to have a baby. They have no place to stay.

Master: Oh, do what you will; just don't bother me.

Sarah: *(To Joseph)* Sir, in the back, go quickly.

Joseph: Thank you, my dear. God bless you.

(Action: Mary and Joseph turn and hurry back to the stable.)

Sarah: *(Returns to the table and pours each guest wine)* Is there anything more I can do for you?

Second Woman: Just leave us alone so we can eat. *(Motions her away)*

(Sarah picks up empty tray and returns to kitchen.)

(Action: Lights dim and people continue to eat and talk softly.)

Music: "Away In A Manger"

(Action: Spotlight goes to Mary holding the baby. Sarah enters stable carrying a tray of food and wine. She sets the tray down next to Mary.)

Mary: God bless you, my child.

Joseph: Thank you, dear girl ... we are truly thankful.

(Sarah looks at baby in Mary's arms.)

Mary: Would you like to hold him?

Sarah: Oh, yes, thank you. *(Lifts the baby and wraps him in her apron to hold him close)*

(Action: Mary and Joseph begin to eat, with Joseph serving Mary.)

(Sarah holds baby tenderly then lays him back into the manger. Sarah sits down on straw next to manger and pats him.)

Music: "While Shepherds Watch Their Flocks By Night"

Narrator: We read in Luke 2:8-9: *"There were some shepherds in that part of the country who were spending the night in the fields, taking care of their flocks. An angel of the Lord appeared to them, and the glory of the Lord shone over them and they were terribly afraid."*

Angel: *(From the side)* I am here with good news, which will bring great joy to all people. This very day, in David's town, your Savior was born; Christ the Lord! And this is what will prove it to you; you will find a baby wrapped in swaddling cloths and lying in a manger.

Narrator: *"Suddenly there was with the angel a multitude of the heavenly host, praising God and saying, 'Glory to God in the highest heaven and on the earth peace among those whom he favors!' "* (Luke 2:13-14).

(Action: Shepherds enter left aisle and walk to front of room. Spotlight goes to Inn door. There is a knock. The guests at the Inn are still eating and chatting at the table, oblivious to the drama taking place in the stable.)

Master: *(Goes to door ... speaks gruffly)* Yes, and what do you want?

Nathan: Greetings, my friend, we are looking for a baby ...

Joram: A baby born this night ...

Master: A baby? There was a couple who came to our door, and she was expecting a baby.

Nathan: May we see them?

Master: There was no room at our Inn.

Joram: *(Alarmed)* Where did they go?

Master: We sent them to the stable ... in the back of the Inn.

Nathan: Thank you, sir.

(Action: Spotlight goes to manger scene as Shepherds enter stable.)

Nathan: Praise the Lord. It is the Messiah ... it is the Messiah.

Ahab: Glory be to God.

Joseph: Welcome to our humble room ... and what brings you here?

Nathan: We were in the field with our sheep ...

Joram: And God's Angels came down from heaven ... and spoke to us.

Ahab: And there were a whole lot of them and they sang to us.

Sarah: What did the Angels say?

Joram: "Glory be to God in the Highest, and on earth, peace to all men."

Nathan: The Angel said, *"Do not be afraid; for see — I am bringing you good news of great joy for all the people. To you is born this day in the city of David a Savior, who is the Messiah, the Lord"* (Luke 2:10-11).

Sarah: Did he say, the Messiah? What makes you think this could be the Messiah?

Joram: The Angel said, *"This will be a sign for you; you will find a child wrapped in bands of cloth and lying in a manger"* (Luke 2:12).

22

Sarah: Oh, the Lord has blessed us ... how the Lord has blessed us.

Music: "Birthday Of A King"

Narrator: As we read in Matthew, *"Come, you that are blessed by my Father, inherit the kingdom prepared for you from the foundation of the world; for I was hungry and you gave me food, I was thirsty and you gave me something to drink, I was a stranger and you welcomed me, I was naked and you gave me clothing, I was sick and you took care of me, I was in prison and you visited me. Truly I tell you, just as you did it to one of the least of these who are members of my family, you did it to me"* (Matthew 25:34-40).

The End

The children of the

present

Blessed

by Doris Wells Miller

"But he said to them: The kings of the Gentiles lord it over them; and those in authority over them are called benefactors. But not so with you; rather the greatest among you must become like the youngest, and the leader like one who serves. For who is greater, the one who is at the table or the one who serves? Is it not the one at the table? But I am among you as one who serves" (Luke 22:25-27).

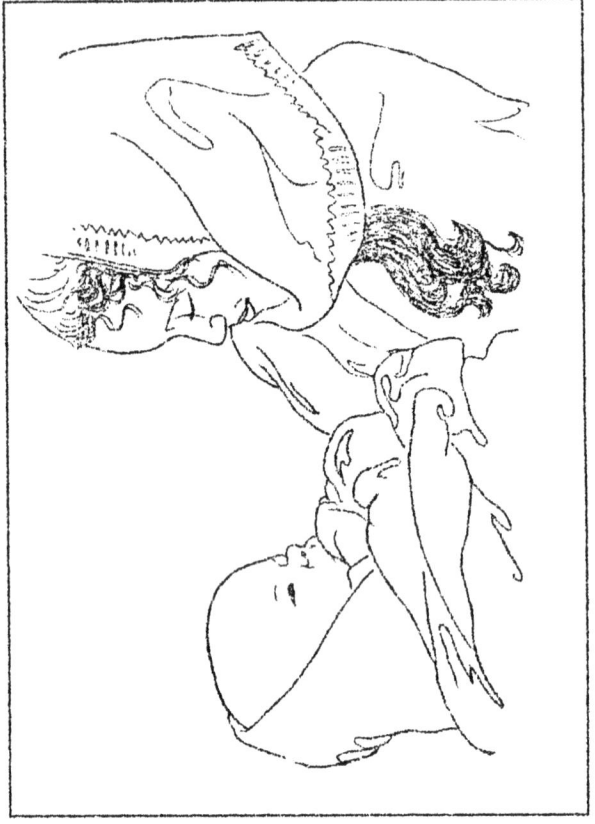

Blessed

The guests at the Inn were concerned with their own affairs, both pleasures and discomforts. The keeper of the Inn was busy with his guests. When the Holy Family arrived at the doorstep of the Inn, the occupants could not see beyond their own needs. But, a young girl, overloaded with work and exhausted, still found room in her heart to see the need of others. She considered their need and found a place where they could stay. While everyone else went about his own business and was interested only in himself, she above all others was the one who was blessed.

At times we are so full of our own need we cannot see the sufferings around us. We are encouraged by this child's example to notice how we can be of help. What blessings await us, for as the scriptures say, *"Truly I tell you, just as you did it to one of the least of these who are members of my family, you did it to me"* (Matthew 25:40).

Jonathan's Cloak

Long before the Bible, as we know it, was written, stories of the Israelites' history and their relationship to God were told by the elders of the tribe. These stories were told and retold and handed down from father to son. The shepherds in the fields carried on this tradition by looking to the eldest in the group to retell these ancient stories. In this play we join a group of Shepherds around their campfire as they spend the night on the hillsides outside Bethlehem. The story of the coming of a Messiah is retold and hope is renewed.

Characters

Narrator	Jonathan
Tobias	Josiah
Amos	Daniel
Samuel	Joseph
Micah	Mary
Ezra	Angel
Very young children as sheep	

Scene One

(Setting: Center stage has a few logs piled up like a campfire. Logs, rocks, or small chairs can be covered with a brown cloth to represent a campsite. Children carry botas or a cup to put water in. If they use a cup, there needs to be a rustic-looking jar with water at the campsite. Each child carries his own food which could be fruit or bread.)

Choir: "The Lord's My Shepherd"

Narrator: Nearly 2,000 years ago shepherds tended their flocks on the hillsides of Judea. As evening descended, they would gather around a campfire to keep warm and eat their evening meal. Then, just as their fathers had done before them, they would relate the history of their people and tell of God's promises.

(Action: Tobias, Amos, Samuel, and Micah enter with their sheep. Each comes from a different area, and walks to campsite and all gather around the campfire. Their sheep lie down beside them. [Sheep are pre-kindergarten children wearing caps with floppy ears. It is permissible for the sheep/children to wander about and baaaaa from time to time, and, yes, it is true, they will often steal the scene.] Ezra and Josiah join the others and greet one another as they prepare the campfire.)

Ezra: *(Approaches the campfire with his sheep)* Greetings, friends! The rain this morning will refresh the pastures.

Tobias: *(Stirs fire with a stick)* Yes, it's been so dry I had begun to fear we would have to move farther north to find pasture and still water for the sheep.

Josiah: The Samaritans along the border are not very friendly of late. It would be dangerous.

Micah: Our Roman rulers are more dangerous, Josiah.

Amos: Here come Jonathan and Daniel. I was beginning to worry about you, my sons.

Jonathan: *(Enters with Daniel and their sheep)* Greetings, Father, we'd taken our flock beyond the creek this morning.

Daniel: *(A very young child)* And the rain made it very deep.

Jonathan: We had to find a shallow place to cross.

Daniel: *(Waves arm outward to denote wide)* It was a long way around.

Amos: Thank God you made it safely.

Instrumental: Flute, guitar, or piano plays softly "The Lord Is My Shepherd"

(Action: Background music continues to play as the shepherds settle around the campfire. They sit on rocks or logs with their sheep by their side. It is good to have each shepherd watch after at least one sheep/child. They take out their bags and eat their bread and fruit. They drink from their cups or flasks. As they eat, Amos, the elder shepherd, begins to tell the old stories.)

Amos: *(Dramatically)* Our prophet Isaiah has said, *"See, the Lord God comes with might, and his arm rules for him; his reward is with him, and his recompense before him"* (Isaiah 40:10).

Tobias: *"He will feed his flock like a shepherd, he will gather the lambs in his arms, and carry them in his bosom, and gently lead the mother sheep"* (Isaiah 40:11).

Jonathan: I'm so glad that God takes care of us. Just as we take care of our sheep.

Ezra: *(Sarcastically)* How can you believe that nonsense?

Josiah: Watch how you speak of God, Ezra.

Ezra: *(Becomes angry and loud)* Do you really think God cares? Here we are paying tribute to those ... Roman tyrants!

Samuel: God does not lie. His promises are forever.

Amos: *(Continues)* *"Here is my servant, whom I uphold, my chosen, in whom my soul delights. I have put my spirit upon him; he will bring forth justice to the nations"* (Isaiah 42:1).

Ezra: *(Sneers)* Just when do you think God will get around to sending this ... this Messiah?

Josiah: Who are we to tell God what to do?

Amos: *(Following a rather uncomfortable silence. Kindly, yet with dignity)* "Do not fear, for I am with you, do not be afraid, for I am your God; I will strengthen you, I will help you, I will uphold you with my victorious right hand" (Isaiah 41:10).

Ezra: Oh, Amos, I'm tired of listening to your old stories. Not one of them have come true. Nonsense, I say, nonsense!

Jonathan: We must believe them, Ezra. We must.

Micah: My dear Jonathan, that is the important thing. Without God, or hope, there is nothing.

Amos: *(After another awkward, uncomfortable silence)* It's late. We must rise early.

(Action: Each Shepherd, in turn, bids good night and settles himself on the ground with his little sheep by his side, pats it and speaks softly to it. Sheep baaaaa from time to time. Lights dim.)

Choir: "O Come, O Come, Emmanuel"

Narrator: Early the next morning they rise and set about their daily tasks.

(Action: Shepherds lead their sheep off stage in different directions. They bid others good day. Daniel and Jonathan move to area on right side. Daniel takes out flute and plays [a real flute could play off stage]. Their sheep move about, nibble at the grass, baaaaa, lie down. From the side aisle, a man and woman move slowly to where the boys are sitting. The woman looks very tired.)

Joseph: Good morning, young men.

Jonathan: Good morning, sir.

Joseph: Could you tell us where we might find a well? We are very thirsty.

Jonathan: There is no well near here. But, here ... you are welcome to drink from our flask.

Joseph: *(Offers drink to Mary)* We thank you very much.

Mary: God bless you, kind friends.

Jonathan: You must have come a long way.

Joseph: Yes, we are from Nazareth. We are going to Bethlehem to register for the taxes.

Daniel: We have seen many people on the road.

Joseph: My wife is with child, and it has been a long hard trip.

(Mary wraps arms about her shoulders and shivers.)

Jonathan: You are cold ... here, take my wrap.

Mary: But, you will need it.

Jonathan: I have another back at camp.

Mary: I am grateful to you, thank you.

Joseph: You have been very kind.

Daniel: Stay and rest under this tree.

Joseph: We must move on if we are to reach Bethlehem before dark.

(Action: The couple move down another aisle. Daniel resumes playing flute.)

Daniel: She was so tired; we should have taken them back to camp.

Jonathan: Bethlehem is just a few miles. They will be there before dark, and it will be better for them to find a warm room.

(Action: The lights begin to dim to denote the end of the day and the Shepherds all return to camp to settle around the campfire, tend their sheep, and greet one another. They take out food to eat, drink, and chat.)

Choir: "O Little Town Of Bethlehem"

Tobias: According to the prophet Ezekiel the Lord says: *"I will save my flock, they shall no longer be ravaged"* (Ezekiel 34:22a).

Amos: *"I will set up over them one shepherd, my servant David, and he shall feed them and be their shepherd"* (Ezekiel 34:23a).

Jonathan: How will we know who this King is when he comes?

Ezra: Even if he does come, which I doubt, do you really think that Herod would allow him to live? You know how jealous he is of his throne. Why, he thinks he is God himself.

Josiah: Do you think that God is so weak he would allow the Messiah to be destroyed before he saves us?

Jonathan: I believe that God will do all that he has promised.

Daniel: I do, too!

(Action: Spot reveals Angel standing near them and they look up in surprise.)

Angel: Do not be afraid!

Samuel: What is happening? Who are you?

Angel: I am here with good news which will bring great joy to all peoples.

Tobias: Good news?

Angel: Today, in Bethlehem, your Savior is born. He is Christ the Lord.

Micah: The Messiah?

Ezra: But — how will we know him? Where will we find him?

Angel: You will find a baby, wrapped in swaddling cloths and lying in a manger.

Choir: "Gloria" (chorus from "Angels We Have Heard On High")

Tobias: Let us go to Bethlehem and see this thing that the Angel has told us.

Ezra: *(Wonderingly, unable to believe what he has heard)* The Messiah? Could it really be the Messiah?

Josiah: At long last!

Jonathan: What are we waiting for? Let's go ...

(Action: Everyone rises and starts to leave ... Daniel struggles to his feet.)

Daniel: Wait for me, wait for me.

(Action: Shepherds leave, going down aisle to back.)

Scene Two

(Setting: Lights dim. The scene is changed from campsite to manger using the same area. Remove campfire, and throw a blanket over the logs or rocks. It would be nice if you could "acquire" a real baby and have Mary hold it; if not, a doll may be used in the manger. Mary and Joseph take their places by the manger.)

Narrator: Excitedly the Shepherds make their way into Bethlehem where they find the stable, come before Mary and Joseph, and kneel in awe of the newborn King.

(Action: Shepherds come up aisle from the back, led by Daniel, Amos, and Tobias; they go to the manger and kneel beside it.)

Tobias: *(To Mary and Joseph)* God's Angel came to us in the fields.

Amos: He told us that we would find a baby wrapped in swaddling cloths and lying in a manger.

Josiah: And that this baby is our Savior, Christ the Lord.

Jonathan: And the Angels were singing, "Glory to God in the Highest Heaven."

Daniel: *(Raises hands and waves them about)* The Angels were all around us.

Mary: "My heart praises the Lord, my soul is glad because of God my Savior."

Ezra: *(Reaches out and touches the cover on the babe)* This cover? ... it ... it looks familiar.

Amos: Why, it looks just like Jonathan's cloak.

Tobias: *(Kindly)* Jonathan, how could it be that the Messiah is warmed by your cloak?

Jonathan: *(Comes near manger, looks at baby tenderly, then speaks to Mary)* You are the people we met on the road yesterday.

Joseph: Yes, my son, your gift has warmed the Christ Child.

(Action: Everyone looks at Jonathan in wonder. Amos puts his arm about him proudly.)

Angel: *(From the side)* "Lord, when was it that we saw you hungry or thirsty or a stranger or naked or sick or in prison, and did not take care of you? Then he will answer them, 'Truly I tell you, just as you did not do it to one of the least of these, you did not do it to me' "* (Matthew 25:44-45).

The End

The children of the

present

Jonathan's Cloak

by Doris Wells Miller

"Lord, when was it that we saw you hungry or thirsty or a stranger or naked or sick or in prison, and did not take care of you? Then he will answer them, 'Truly I tell you, just as you did not do it to one of the least of these, you did not do it to me' " (Matthew 25:44-45).

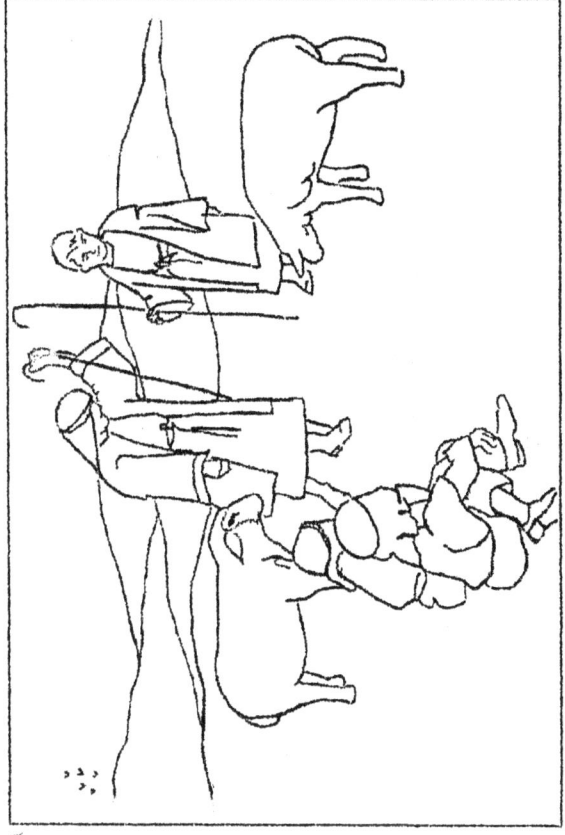

Jonathan's Cloak

Long before the Bible, as we know it, was written, stories of the Israelites' history and their relationship to God were told by the elders of the tribe. These stories were told and retold and handed down from father to son. The shepherds in the fields carried on this tradition by looking to the eldest in the group to retell these ancient stories. In this play we join a group of Shepherds around their campfire as they spend the night on the hillsides outside Bethlehem. The story of the coming of a Messiah is retold and hope is renewed.

Proclamation

"For a child has been born for us, a son given to us; authority rests upon his shoulders and he is named Wonderful Counselor, Prince of Peace." — Isaiah 9:6

This production was written with older children in mind. It is a way to encourage each child to research the character that he or she is to portray and to tell us something about who he or she is representing. The players will design their own costumes using their research. Work on this play needs to be started several months before the program to give participants time to do the research.

Characters

Storyteller	Isaiah
Mary	Gabriel
Emperor Augustus	Innkeeper
Angel	Angel Two
Angel Three	Shepherd
Choir	

Choir: "We've A Story To Tell To The Nations"

(Action: The Storyteller sits on a rocker which is elevated at the front of sanctuary. There is a large Bible on a stand next to chair. Storyteller is relaxed, smiles, and greets audience.)

Storyteller: *(Lifts large Bible and places it in lap. Turns pages thoughtfully till he finds his place)* Good evening, children, Mothers, Fathers, and friends. We have a story to tell you. So sit back and relax.

Long, long ago, in a land far away, in the land of Judah, there lived a great prophet whose name was Isaiah. Now, Isaiah listened to what God said to him and tried to tell others God's message. Now, this was not a good time for the people of Judah as there was a cruel King that was threatening them, and the people were very frightened.

(Action: Isaiah walks slowly up the aisle to side stage. He is a bent old man in flowing robes. As he walks, he stops several times to gaze over the audience as if to understand them.)

Isaiah: *(From his research, student describes Isaiah [Helps: Isaiah 6])* Isaiah was a prophet of God. He told his people that God was more powerful than their King and that their real problem was that they did not trust God enough. He also told them that God would send a special King (the Messiah) who would bring peace to all the world.

Isaiah: *(Possible dialogue)* Dear friends. God said, "A child is born to us! A son is given and he will be our ruler. He will be called, 'Wonderful Counselor, Mighty God, Eternal Father, Prince of Peace.' His royal power will grow and his kingdom will be at peace. He will rule like King David with right and justice for all time. The Lord Almighty has spoken."

(Action: After Isaiah speaks, he makes his way over to the center stage where Storyteller is sitting and sits on a chair near the base of the elevated stage.)

Storyteller: Many years later God sent the angel Gabriel to a town in Galilee named Nazareth. He had a message for a girl promised in marriage to Joseph, who was a descendant of King David. The girl's name was Mary.

(Action: Mary walks quietly up the aisle and sits on a chair to side of stage. She is wearing soft flowing clothes of a light color.)

Mary: *(Tells about herself* [Helps: Matthew 1:18-24 and Luke 1:26-38]*)* Mary was the mother of Jesus who is the promised Savior, the one through whom God fulfilled the promises he made to his people in the Old Testament.

(Action: Gabriel appears suddenly on right side stage. He is wearing a simple pure white robe.)

Gabriel: *(Tells about himself* [Helps: Luke 1:26-38]*)* Gabriel was an angel of God who spoke directly with people on earth.

Gabriel: *(Calls softly, gently)* Mary, Mary.

Mary: *(Surprised ... opens eyes wide)* What? Who calls me?

Gabriel: Peace be with you! The Lord is with you and has greatly blessed you!

(Mary is deeply troubled and a bit frightened. Mary shrinks back in her chair and looks around. Then she looks questioningly at the Angel.)

Gabriel: Don't be afraid, Mary; God has been gracious to you.

Mary: Are you God's messenger? Are you an angel?

Gabriel: You will become pregnant and give birth to a son, and you will name him Jesus.

Mary: Me? A son?

Gabriel: He will be called the Son of the Most High God and he will be the king of the descendants of Jacob forever; his kingdom will never end.

Mary: But, I am a virgin. How can this be?

Gabriel: The Holy Spirit will come to you, and God's power will rest upon you. For this reason the holy child will be called the Son of God.

Mary: *(Stands, as if in awe)* I am the Lord's servant. May it happen to me as you have said.

(Gabriel departs as suddenly as he appeared.)

(Mary, quietly and thoughtfully, sits down on the chair.)

Storyteller: At that time, Emperor Augustus ordered a census to be taken throughout the Roman Empire.

Emperor Augustus: *(Tells about himself* [Helps: Luke 2:1-3]*)* About 27 B.C., Augustus assumed the rank of emperor of Rome. The city of Rome was truly the center of the civilized world.

Emperor Augustus: *(Possible dialogue)* Citizens of Rome, Servants of the Holy Roman Empire, slaves and free men. I have decreed that a census be taken, a count of every man, woman and child. People of Judea, you are to go to the town from which your family originated. I will send a centurion who will record your names. This will be done under penalty of death.

Storyteller: Everyone went to register himself, each to his own hometown. Joseph went from the town of Nazareth in Galilee to the town of Bethlehem in Judea, the birthplace of King David because he was a descendant of David. Mary, who was promised in marriage to him, went with him. She was pregnant, and while they were in Bethlehem, the time came for her to have her baby.

Innkeeper: *(Innkeeper tells about himself* [Helps: Luke 2:1-7]*)* The Innkeeper represents the owner of the Inn who, the Bible does not say, either turned the holy couple away in their time of need *or* offered them the stable when he had no other place for them.

Innkeeper: *(Possible dialogue)* I am the Innkeeper in Bethlehem, a small village in Judea. As was my custom, I would stand at the door of the Inn toward evening and watch as people walked past on the roadway. Many people were arriving to register for the taxes because it was the home of their ancestors.

It was beginning to get dark and cold. The Inn had been filled much earlier in the day. Every room contained several families. In one room we had twenty people scattered across the floor. I would have to tell each new traveler to move on even though I knew many would have to spend the night on the cold ground against the city wall. Then, I saw this young couple. She was riding on a small donkey and her husband looked as if he had walked for many miles. There was no room, but my heart went out to her — she was so tired and obviously very pregnant. *(Pauses)* There was something very special about the couple. I thought about the stable at the back of the Inn. It was really just a cave where we kept the animals, but it would be shelter for this man and woman. *(Walks slowly over to the elevated stage and takes his place on a lower step)*

(Action: After the Innkeeper speaks, the Storyteller picks up his Bible and comes quietly to the chair previously occupied by Mary. Mary gets up and sits in rocking chair holding baby.)

Storyteller: And while they were in Bethlehem, the time came for Mary to have her baby and she gave birth to her first son, wrapped him in swaddling cloths and laid him in a manger, for there was no room for them to stay in the Inn.

(Action: Light comes on Mary and the baby. She rocks baby.)

Choir: "What Child Is This?"

Storyteller: There were some Shepherds in that part of the country who were spending the night in the fields, taking care of their flocks. An Angel of the Lord appeared to them, and the glory of the Lord shone over them. They were terribly afraid.

Angel: *(Tells about him/herself* [Helps: Luke 2:8-14]*)* God's angels were seen and heard by the Shepherds as they rejoiced at the birth of God's son.

Angel: Don't be afraid! I come with good news of great joy to all the people. This very day in David's town your Savior was born ... Christ the Lord. And this is what will prove it to you: you will find a baby wrapped in swaddling cloths and lying in a manger.

Angel Two: *(Stands next to Angel)* Glory to God in the highest heaven.

Angel Three: And peace on earth to all.

(Action: Angels take their place in the back of Mary.)

Storyteller: Suddenly, a great army of heaven's angels appeared and began to sing praises to God:

Choir: Chorus of "Gloria" from "Angels We Have Heard On High"

(Action: Several children, dressed as Shepherds, come forward and take their places on the higher steps of the elevated stage.)

Shepherd: *(Shepherd tells about himself* [Helps: Luke 2:8-20]*)* It was the custom in those days for men to stay out in the fields to protect the sheep.

Storyteller: When the angels went away from them, the Shepherds said to one another, "Let's go to Bethlehem and see this thing that has happened, which the Lord has told us." So they hurried off and found Mary and Joseph and saw the baby lying in the manger. When the Shepherds saw him, they told them what the Angel had said about the child. All who heard it were amazed at what the Shepherds said. Mary remembered all these things and thought deeply about them.

Gabriel:
When the song of the angel is stilled,
When the star in the sky is gone,
When the kings and princes are home,
When the shepherds are back with their flock,
The work of Christmas begins:
To find the lost, To heal the broken,
To feed the hungry, To release the prisoner,
To rebuild the nations, To bring peace among brothers,
To make music in the heart.*

The End

*Written by Howard Thurman, from the *Mood of Christmas* (HarperCollins).

The children of the

present

Proclamation

by Doris Wells Miller

"For a child has been born for us, a son given to us; authority rests upon his shoulders and he is named Wonderful Counselor, Prince of Peace" (Isaiah 9:6).

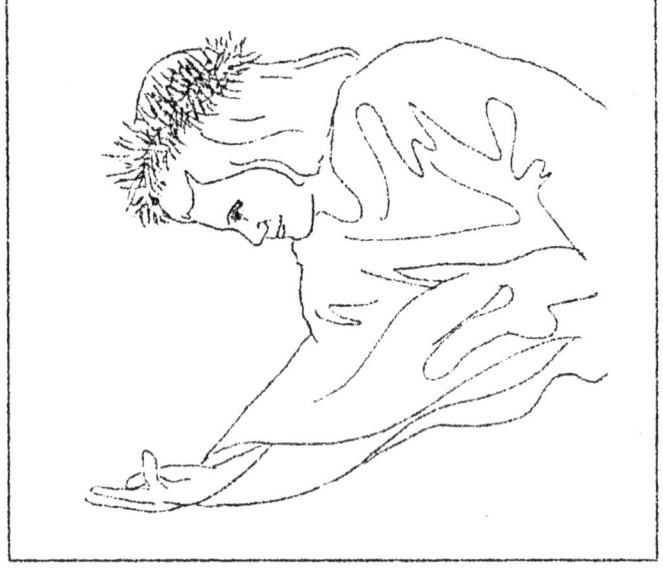

Proclamation

This production was written with older children in mind. It is a way to encourage each child to research the character that he or she portrays and to tell us something about who he or she is representing. The players designed their own costumes using their research. Work on this play started several months before the program to give participants time to do the research.

The Big Picture

"So they went with haste and found Mary and Joseph, and the child lying in the manger."
—Luke 2:16

Like a rendering of one of the old masterpieces of the Nativity by a famous artist, we see each person in the Christmas story come alive and tell you his version of what happened that special night when Christ was born and then take their place in the picture so they all come together to form a portrait. Come, see and hear what happened from the perspective of the people who could have been there.

Characters
Reader

Cornelius *(Census taker)*

Jotham *(Innkeeper)*

Samuel *(Stable boy)*

Joseph

Mary

Miriam *(Midwife)*

Angel

Nathan *(Shepherd)*

Stephen *(Shepherd)*

Baby Jesus *(doll)*

(Setting: The reader stands on the left side front. Each participant, in turn, walks down the center aisle from the back of the room to a microphone at the front right side of the stage. Following each presentation each takes his assigned place on stage [or in the case of the Innkeeper and Census taker, by the door to the Bethlehem Inn]. The manger scene could be center stage and the door to the Bethlehem Inn on the far left to indicate that the Innkeeper and Census taker really were not part of the Nativity.)

Reader: "Thou Didst Leave Thy Throne" (a reading by Emily E. S. Elliott, 1864)
Thou didst leave Thy throne and Thy kingly crown
when Thou camest to earth for me;
but in Bethlehem's home there was found no room,
For Thy holy nativity.
Heaven's arches rang when the angels sang,
Proclaiming Thy royal degree;
But in lowly birth Thou didst come to earth,
And in great humility:
come to my heart, Lord Jesus!
there is room in my heart for Thee.

Choir: "Birthday Of A King"

Census taker: *(Enters center aisle, reads from a scroll and proclaims loudly)* Listen, all you citizens and servants of the Holy Roman Empire. By decree of our mighty Emperor, Caesar Augustus, a census will be taken throughout all of the Roman Empire. Each man shall return to the place of his forefathers so that an accurate count may be made of every person in this land. *(Lowers scroll)*

(Speaks softly to audience as if in conversation) Greetings, my name is Cornelius. I am a soldier in Caesar Augustus' Royal Army. I have been sent to Bethlehem to be the official registrar of all the Israelite

37

people who are of the line of Jesse. I have been staying at the Bethlehem Inn, over there *(Points to doorway on left stage)*, for the last three weeks and will probably be here several weeks more. I will be glad when this work is finished and I can return to my home and family in Rome. To be honest with you ... this is not my idea of a soldier's duty. Except for the Innkeeper, the people in this village are not very happy to see me. *(Walks to doorway of Bethlehem Inn)*

Innkeeper: *(Enters up center aisle)* Good evening, my friends. My name is Jotham. I am the master of the Bethlehem Inn. There is but one Inn in this small village and, because of this busy time, my establishment shall be known all over Israel. All the rooms have been filled every night. With my wise planning and use of my neighbors' produce, there is no doubt that I shall become a very wealthy man. This has been the best thing that has ever happened to our village. *(Walks over and takes his place beside Roman soldier at door of Inn. They chat quietly)*

Samuel: *(Enters up center aisle)* Me? *(Points to self questioningly)* I don't have long to talk to you tonight. *(Counts on fingers)* Let's see. There are three donkeys, a goat, two cows, and some chickens that depend on me to keep them fed and their straw clean. Oh, my name is Samuel and I am the stable boy for the Bethlehem Inn. Yes, I am young for this job, but since Mother passed away and Father is in the fields with the sheep, it gives me a place to sleep. I get the leftovers from the kitchen and the best part is that it gives me some denari for my pocket. *(Pats side)* So, all in all, I am very fortunate. Now, I must get going, there's a lot of work to be done. *(Goes to stable and starts to rake the straw)*

(Action: Joseph and Mary arrive together.)

Joseph: Greetings, friends. I am Joseph, and this is my wife Mary. Our home is in Nazareth far to the north, and we have been walking the dusty roads for many days.

Mary: Good to meet you. Yes, for many days our dear little donkey has patiently carried me over many miles of dangerous terrain. We are very tired.

Joseph: This trip came at a bad time for Mary. She is expecting her first child, but we had no choice. *(Shakes head sadly)* Caesar has decreed that we must return to the city of our forefathers. We are descendants of David, the line of Jesse, so this is what we must do.

Mary: I have been so worried that the baby would be born on the roadside. Thank God, we made it safely to Bethlehem before dark. Now, all we need to do is find a warm room.

Joseph: It was good meeting you, but we must be entering the village before dark.

(Action: They walk over to the Inn door and speak with the Innkeeper who indicates by motions that there is no room in the Inn.)

Miriam: *(Carries water jug on shoulder)* Oh, good day to you. I am Miriam, the Innkeeper's wife. I'm on my way to the well. With all the guests at the Inn, it feels like all I do is go to the well for water. We are not the only place that is full, every household has family visiting or they have taken in guests. I've even seen people sleeping under trees next to the village wall. It must be hard for them as the nights have been very cold. *(Walks down side aisle to unseen well)*

(Action: Joseph and Mary slowly and sadly return to center stage.)

Joseph: No, we are not leaving the village, we cannot. But the Inn is full and there is no place for us to stay. It looks as if we will have to bed down at the village gate.

Mary: Oh, Joseph, what shall we do? ... I fear the baby is due, and it is too cold without shelter.

Samuel: *(Returns to center stage)* Greetings, friends. Are you just arriving so late in the day?

Joseph: Greetings, young man. We have been in the village a few hours, but we have been unable to locate any kind of room for the night.

Mary: Would you know of any place we could stay? We are desperate. My baby will come soon, and I fear the cold night air.

Samuel: I know of no warm room. *(Pauses to think)* But I sleep in the cave over there. It is my job to tend the animals. The straw is soft and the cave gives shelter from the cold wind. I could move over and make room for you. And, oh yes, there is a place for your donkey too.

Joseph: Thank you, my boy. Yes, thank you.

Mary: God bless you, young man. We are very grateful.

Samuel: Here is the doorway. You go on in, and I will run and find Miriam, the midwife.

(Action: Mary and Joseph go into the stable. Samuel leaves to find Miriam.)

Reader: "Gentle Mary Laid Her Child" (a reading by Joseph Simpson Cook, 1919)
Gentle Mary laid her Child Lowly in a manger;
There He lay, the Undefiled, To the world a stranger.
Such a babe in such a place, Can He be the Savior?
Ask the saved of all the race Who have found his favor.

(Action: Samuel and Miriam hurry up side aisle to stable.)

Angel: *(Stands off to side)* Don't be afraid! I am here with good news, which will bring great joy to all people. This very day in David's town your Savior is born — Christ the Lord! And this is what will prove it to you. You will find a baby wrapped in cloths and lying in a manger.

(Action: While the Angel speaks, Mary takes doll from hiding place behind her chair and places it in the manger. The Angel goes to stand behind and above manger scene. Two Shepherds enter down center aisle.)

Nathan: Where is he? Where is he?

Stephen: Do you know where the child is? The one that was born tonight?

Nathan: Oh, I'm Nathan, and this is Stephen. We were out on the hillside with our sheep and the strangest thing happened.

Stephen: The night was so still ... the sky very dark. But the stars were more bright than I can ever remember. Especially, a big one overhead ... one that I've never seen before.

Nathan: There was this sound, like the wind blowing, but it wasn't ... There was no breeze. It sounded, it sounded almost like someone ... someone singing.

Stephen: My hair stood up straight ... It was like I was chilled ... but I wasn't cold. It was scary.

Nathan: I looked and there was this Angel. Yes, an Angel said, "Don't be afraid."

Stephen: But, I was ... you can be sure of that.

Nathan: The Angel told us that the Messiah, Christ our Lord, was born tonight and that we would find him in Bethlehem, lying in a manger.

Stephen: We left our sheep in the care of Timothy and hurried into the village to find our Savior.

Nathan: Tell us, do you know where we might find him?

Stephen: The stable? Of course, we'll find a manger there. *(Motions to audience)* Come, let's go.

(Action: Shepherds go to manger and bow before Jesus and become part of manger scene. Innkeeper and soldier continue to chat in doorway.)

Angel: Glory be to God in the highest heaven and peace on earth to all men.

Mary: My heart praises the Lord. My soul is glad because of God my Savior.

Miriam: How blessed we are to see the Messiah with our own eyes.

Samuel: Yes, we are blessed. But, how much more blessed are they who come after us and do not see him, yet believe.

(Action: All participants remain in their places without moving to simulate the portrait. You could invite the audience to come forward and take pictures.)

The End

The children of the

present

The Big Picture

by Doris Wells Miller

"So they went with haste and found Mary and Joseph, and the child lying in the manger" (Luke 2:16).

The Big Picture

Like a rendering of one of the old masterpieces of the Nativity by a famous artist, we see each person in the Christmas story come alive and tell you his version of what happened that special night when Christ was born and then each takes his place in the picture so they all come together to form a portrait. Come, see and hear what happened from the perspective of the people who could have been there.

The Christmas Story

"While they were there, the time came for her to deliver her child. And she gave birth to her first-born son and wrapped him in bands of cloth, and laid him in a manger, because there was no place for them in the Inn."   —Luke 2:6-7

Mother and Father gather their children around them, open the Bible, and read the Christmas story. The children are dressed appropriately to take their places in the Nativity scene as their parts are read. While the story is read, the children have an opportunity to share their feelings about what it must have been like to have lived in that time. When the story ends, the manger scene is complete.

Characters

Mother	First Reader
Father	Second Reader
Joseph	Angels
Mary	Shepherds

(Setting: Elevated at left center stage is a manger scene consisting of a small chair and an empty manger. There is no special lighting. At stage right is an easy chair and a rocking chair and a small Christmas tree, or candle decoration. Mother and Father gather the children around them. Mother sits in the rocking chair holding the youngest, and Father sits in the easy chair with a large Bible on his lap. The children are in their costumes.)

Mother: Gather close, my children, so we can hear Father read this special story from the Bible about the very first Christmas.

Father: *(Ceremoniously opens the large Bible in his lap. Turns to the page with a book mark)* Tonight, my children, we will read from Luke 2. This is a special story that tells us what this holiday is all about. *(Reads)* *"In those days a decree went out from Emperor Augustus that all the world should be registered. Joseph also went from the town of Nazareth in Galilee to Judea, to the city of David called Bethlehem, because he was descended from the house and family of David. He went to be registered with Mary, to whom he was engaged and who was expecting a child"* (Luke 2:1-5).

Mother: Bethlehem was a small village, a town where the shepherds and their families lived. Many people had come into town in order to register for the taxes, but, the town had only one Inn, and it was full to overflowing.

Choir: "Oh, Little Town Of Bethlehem" (one verse)

(Action: As the children sing, Joseph and Mary [in costume] rise from the group of children and take their places at the manger scene. Mary is carrying a baby doll wrapped in swaddling cloths.)

Mother and Father and Children: *(Ad lib)* Talk with the children about Bethlehem. Talk about why the people had to travel to their hometown and about how crowded it was. Have you ever been so tired that you couldn't take another step? Think about how tired Joseph and Mary must have been after their hard trip.

Father: *(Reads)* *"While they were there, the time came for her to deliver her child. And she gave birth to her firstborn son and wrapped him in bands of cloth, and laid him in a manger, because there was no place for them in the inn"* (Luke 2:6-7).

(Action: Spotlight goes to manger. Mary lays the baby doll in the manger.)

Mother: The only place they could find to stay was in a stable where baby Jesus' crib was a manger, a place where straw and seeds were kept to feed the animals. Humble as it was, the straw was soft and warm and the stable sheltered them from the cold winds.

Mother and Father and Children: *(Ad lib)* Have you ever seen inside of a barn where they keep animals? The place where they put the feed is a called a manger. Is that a nice clean bed for a baby? You could talk about how cold it must have been and how hard it was to keep a tiny baby warm and comfortable.

Children: "Away In A Manger"

Father: *(Reads)* *"In that region there were shepherds living in the field, keeping watch over their flock by night"* (Luke 2:8).

Children: "While Shepherds Watched Their Flocks By Night"

Mother and Father and Children: *(Ad lib)* Does anyone know what a shepherd is? Have you ever seen a sheep? *(Encourage children to talk about their own experiences in camping out)*

(Shepherds get up and go to a place on the far side of the manger scene.)

(An Angel walks over to stand at the side of Shepherds with arms raised.)

Father: *(Reads)* *"Then an angel of the Lord stood before them, and the glory of the Lord shone around them, and they were terrified. But the angel said to them, 'Do not be afraid, for see — I am bringing you good news of great joy for all the people: to you is born this day in the city of David, a Savior, who is the Messiah, the Lord'"* (Luke 2:9-11).

(The rest of the Angels join the first Angel around the Shepherds.)

First Reader: "The First Noel" (arranged by John Stainer, 1871, a reading)
   The first Noel the angel did say was to certain poor shepherds in fields as they lay,
   In fields where they lay keeping their sheep, on a cold winter's night that was so deep.
   Noel, Noel, Noel, born is the King of Israel.

Father: *(Reads)* *"This will be a sign for you; you will find a child wrapped in bands of cloth and lying in a manger. And suddenly there was with the angel a multitude of the heavenly host, praising God and saying, 'Glory to God in the highest heaven, and on earth peace among those whom he favors'"* (Luke 2:12-14).

(Children dressed as Angels circle around Mary, Joseph, and the baby and finally stand behind them with half of the group on each side of manger scene.)

(Action: More lights are turned onto Angels.)

Children: "Angels We Have Heard On High" (one verse and chorus)

Mother and Father and Children: *(Ad lib)* Imagine what it must have been like to have angels everywhere singing just to you.

Father: *(Reads)* *"When the angels had left them and gone into heaven, the shepherds said to one another, 'Let us go now to Bethlehem and see this thing that has taken place, which the Lord has made known to us' "* (Luke 2:15).

(Action: Shepherds and Angels go to the manger scene with Shepherds kneeling before the manger and the Angels gathering around behind.)

Father: *"So they went with haste and found Mary and Joseph, and the child lying in the manger. When they saw this, they made known that which had been told them about this child; and all who heard it were amazed at what the shepherds told them"* (Luke 2:16-17).

Second Reader: "Once In Royal David's City" (a reading by Henry Gauntlett, 1849)
   Once in royal David's city stood a lowly cattle shed
   Where a mother laid her baby, in a manger for his bed:
   Mary was that mother mild, Jesus Christ her little child.

   He came down to earth from heaven, who is God and Lord of all,
   And his shelter was a stable, and his cradle was a stall;
   With the poor, and mean and lowly, lived on earth our Savior Holy.

Mother: *"But Mary treasured all these words and pondered them in her heart"* (Luke 2:19).

The End

The children of

present

The Christmas Story

by Doris Wells Miller

"While they were there, the time came for her to deliver her child. And she gave birth to her firstborn son and wrapped him in bands of cloth, and laid him in a manger, because there was no place for them in the inn" (Luke 2:6-7).

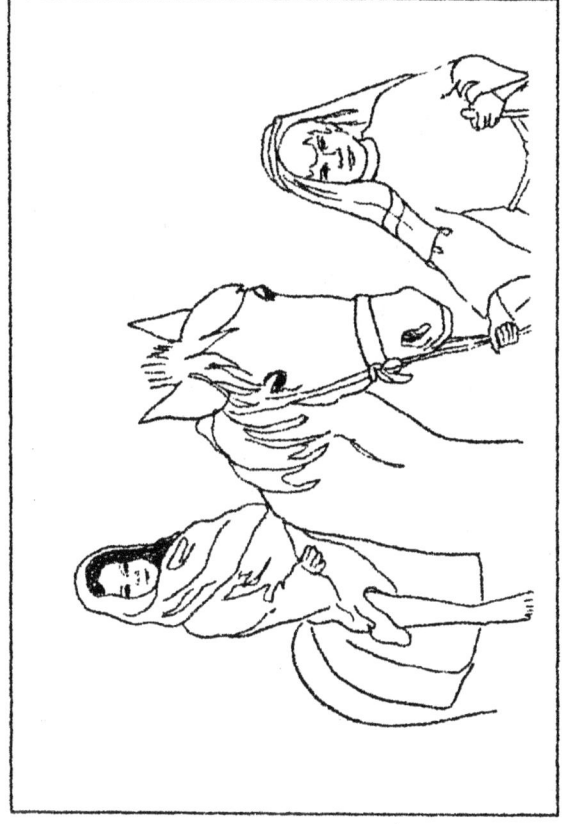

The Christmas Story

Mother and Father gather their children around them, open the Bible, and read the Christmas story. The children are dressed appropriately to take their places in the Nativity scene as their parts are read. While the story is read, the children have an opportunity to share their feelings about what it must have been like to have lived in that time. When the story ends, the manger scene is complete.

The Shawl

"Now in Joppa there was a disciple whose name was Tabitha, which in Greek is Dorcas. She was devoted to good works and acts of charity." — Acts 9:36

Tabitha, who was spoken of so lovingly by her neighbors in Acts 9, was not always such a generous, loving person. When she was a young girl, she was a vain, self-centered child. But an encounter with the Christ Child changed her life dramatically. When she discovered Jesus sleeping in the humble stable, cold and helpless, her heart was changed and she no longer thought only of herself but offered him her most prized possession in order that he might be warm. It was at this point she began to enlarge her view of life and how she could be of help with those in need.

Charactors

Narrator
Amos *(Father, Shepherd)*
Lydia *(Mother)*
Tabitha *(Young girl)*
Anna *(Tabitha's friend)*
Jotham *(Innkeeper)*

Jacob *(Innkeeper's son)*
Joseph
Mary
Baby
Aaron *(Shepherd)*
Philip *(Shepherd)*

Scene One

(Setting: The scene takes place in three areas: Stage left is the Shepherd's home. Lydia is at the table cutting bread and cheese and placing them in a small cloth bag. Tabitha is working at a small loom. Amos comes in with a knapsack. Center stage is the stable. A crude divider stands near the back which indicates the goat stall with a small manger standing at the front to indicate side of stable. Stage right is the Inn door. Outside the door there are pots on a table which Jotham and Jacob are washing.)

Children's Choir: "The Birthday Of A King" (first verse)

Narrator: Many years ago in the village of Bethlehem lived a Shepherd and his family. Amos tended a flock of sheep known for their fine long silky wool. His wife Lydia would spin the wool and weave it into lovely garments. Their daughter, Tabitha, young as she was, already showed great promise of being a fine weaver too. Let us join the family as Amos is preparing to leave for the fields in order to tend the sheep.

(Action: Amos is busy packing a knapsack while Lydia prepares food for him. Tabitha is busy at her loom.)

Lydia: There, that should be enough food to keep you for at least three days, Amos.

Amos: I don't plan to be on the hillside any longer than two nights. It's getting cold.

Lydia: Be sure to take your new cloak I just made; it will be quite warm.

(Action: Shepherds arrive at the door. Amos puts on cloak.)

Aaron: Time to be on our way, Amos.

Amos: Greetings, Aaron and Philip. I'm ready. *(Turns to Lydia)* Take care now, my dear family. If you need me, you can find us on the hills northwest of Bethlehem.

Lydia: Farewell, my dear Amos. We shall be just fine.

Tabitha: Oh, Father, bring back some wool from the black spotted lamb. I need some for the belt I plan to weave.

Amos: Certainly, Tabitha, I'll bring a large sack full. The shawl you are making is just lovely; you are doing a fine job. Someday you will weave better than your mother.

Tabitha: I am planning on it.

(Action: Father and Shepherds leave.)

Lydia: Tabitha, would you give me a hand spinning the raw wool?

Tabitha: Oh, Mother, how can I? My shawl is almost finished; I need only to tie a few ends.

(Action: Anna comes to the door.)

Anna: Greetings, everyone. Tabitha, it is time to go to the stable to milk our goats.

Lydia: Good morning, Anna. We almost forgot about milking the goats, what with getting Amos off to the hills this morning.

Tabitha: *(Takes shawl from loom and lays it around her shoulders)* There, it's all finished. How does it look?

Anna: Oh, Tabitha, it is so beautiful.

Tabitha: Thank you.

Anna: Get your milk jar and let's go.

Tabitha: Mother, where did you put my milk jar?

Lydia: There, in the corner.

Tabitha: Will you get it for me, Mother?

Lydia: *(Wearily picks up jar and hands it to Tabitha)* Now run along, girls. Your lunch will be waiting when you return, my dear.

Tabitha: Here, Anna, will you carry the jar for me? I don't want to soil my new shawl.

(Action: Anna places her jar on her head and takes the other jar in her arms as they leave for the stable.)

Anna: Oh, Tabitha, would you make me a shawl like yours? It is the most beautiful one I have ever seen.

Tabitha: I might, if you will pay me for it.

(Action: The girls go into the stable.)

Scene Two

Narrator: In order to make an accurate count of all the people in his empire, Emperor Augustus Caesar has decreed that everyone must return to the home of his ancestors to be registered for the taxes. The tiny town of Bethlehem is full to overflowing. The Innkeeper, Jotham, and his son Jacob are busy washing the pots and pans used in cooking for the many guests.

Jacob: Father, I'm so tired of washing pots and pans.

Jotham: I am too, Jacob. We have never had so many guests before. Just as soon as one leaves another comes.

(Action: The girls go to the wash table with their milk jars on their heads.)

Anna: Greetings. We have some fresh creamy goat milk. Would you be needing some?

Jotham: Greetings, girls. Yes, we certainly will. The Inn is full, and we are running short of food. I'll gladly pay for all you can bring in.

Tabitha: *(Wrinkles up her nose)* The stable's full of donkeys, and it is beginning to smell awful.

Jotham: Yes, it must be dirty by now. Jacob, do get back to the stable soon and clean it up.

Jacob: Yes, Father. At least it will be a change from washing these pots.

Jotham: Would you girls like to stay and help out with the chores? I will pay you. We have many guests, and we could use some help.

Tabitha: I really don't want to. I plan to start weaving my new belt.

Jotham: You certainly are learning fast. Did you weave that lovely shawl?

Tabitha: Yes.

Jotham: It is just beautiful.

Anna: I would be glad to stay and help. Perhaps I can make enough money to pay Tabitha to make a shawl for me.

48

(Action: Girls set their jars on the ground. Tabitha leaves. Anna starts to wash the pots. Jacob goes into the stable.)

Narrator: Later that evening, among the stream of people arriving in Bethlehem, there is a man and young woman. The woman is very pregnant. They have stopped at every house and Inn on their way into town, but all have turned them away. The young couple wearily comes to the door of the Bethlehem Inn.

Jotham: And what would you be wanting?

Joseph: A room, sir, just a small warm room would do us fine.

Jotham: Be on your way. We are full.

Mary: Oh, kind sir, we are so tired. Have you nowhere we could stay?

Jotham: *(Motions them away)* You heard me. We have no more rooms.

Joseph: Have mercy, sir, it is late. All of the inns are full and my wife is expecting. I fear that she will not be able to travel any further.

(Action: Anna goes to the door of the Inn.)

Anna: Oh, sir, she is so tired. Could they not stay in the stable? My goat stall is warm, and the straw would make a soft bed.

Jotham: Very well. Go, take them with you.

(Action: Anna shows the tired couple to the stable. She spreads her apron on the straw, then leaves them to return to her home.)

Children's Choir: "Silent Night, Holy Night"

Narrator: Meanwhile, out in the fields, the Angel of the Lord has announced to the Shepherds that the blessed event has occurred. God's son, the Messiah, has been born and the Angels sang: "Alleluia, Christ is born, Peace on Earth to all men of good will."

Choir: "Alleluia" from the chorus of "Angels We Have Heard On High"

(Action: Tabitha enters, carrying her milk pot on her head.)

Tabitha: Oh, I didn't know anyone was here. Why are you in the stable?

Joseph: Good morning. The Inn was full and we needed a place to sleep.

Mary: The good Innkeeper said we could sleep on the warm hay.

Tabitha: If you must. I need to milk my goat.

49

(Action: Tabitha walks through the stable to the back. Mary picks up the baby from the manger and holds him. A little later Tabitha comes back with her full milk pot. She stops, wide-eyed, as she sees the baby.)

Tabitha: *(Stops and stares)* A baby?

Mary: Yes, he was born last night.

Tabitha: *(Gently)* May I hold him? *(Puts milk pot on the floor)*

Mary: *(Hands her baby)* Of course. Here.

Tabitha: *(Holds baby tenderly ... touches his little hand)* He, he ... why, he's cold.

Joseph: We wrapped him in swaddling cloths. That is all that we had with us.

Choir: *(Hums softly in background)* "Mary Had A Baby"

Narrator: Tabitha's heart was strangely touched. A tear ran down her cheek as she cuddled the baby closer. Then, as she sat on the floor, she laid the baby in her lap and slipped the beautiful new shawl from her shoulders, gently wrapped it around the baby, and handed him back to his mother. Mary held the baby close and thanked the little girl. Tabitha picked up the milk jar, handed it to Joseph, and walked out quietly.

Choir: *(Sings)* "Mary Had A Baby"

(Action: Joseph pours milk into a cup and hands it to Mary. As Tabitha steps out of the stable, she meets the Shepherds coming in from the fields.)

Amos: Greetings, Tabitha.

Tabitha: Why, Father, what brings you back so soon?

Philip: Greetings, Tabitha. Do you know of a baby born this night? We were told we would find him lying in a manger.

Tabitha: Here in the stable is a baby ... born last night.

Narrator: All enter and bow before the mother and baby. They tell her about the Angel of the Lord and his message.

Tabitha: The Messiah?

Aaron: Yes, the Son of God.

Amos: What is that the Christ Child is wrapped in? Tabitha, it looks like the shawl you made.

Tabitha: Yes, Father, I gave it to the baby; he was cold.

Amos: That was very kind of you, Tabitha. I am proud; you did a fine thing.

Tabitha: That's all right. I can make another. I think I'll make one to give to Anna, too.

Narrator: And, years later, as we read in Acts 9:36-42, when Peter was asked to help Tabitha, her friends told him how she spent all her time doing good and helping the poor. Her friends crowded around Peter and showed him the shirts and coats that Tabitha had made for them and begged Peter to help her.

The End

The children of

present

The Shawl

by Doris Wells Miller

"Now in Joppa there was a disciple whose name was Tabitha, which in Greek is Dorcas. She was devoted to good works and acts of charity" (Acts 9:36).

The Shawl

Tabitha, who was spoken of so lovingly by her neighbors in Acts 9, was not always such a generous, loving person. When she was a young girl, she was a vain, self-centered child. But an encounter with the Christ Child changed her life dramatically. When she discovered Jesus sleeping in the humble stable, cold and helpless, her heart was changed and she no longer thought only of herself but offered him her most prized possession in order that he might be warm. It was at this point she began to enlarge her view of life and how she could be of help with those in need.

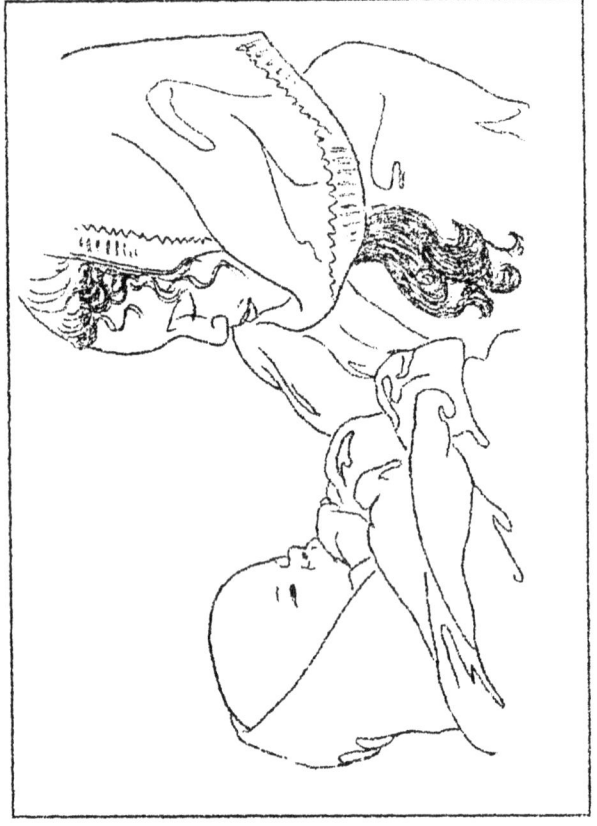

You Are There

Script to be used with slides and Children's Choir

"Greetings, favored one! The Lord is with you. Do not be afraid, Mary, for you have found favor with God. And now, you will conceive in your womb and bear a son, and you will name him Jesus. He will be great, and will be called the Son of the Most High, and the Lord God will give to him the throne of his ancestor David. He will reign over the house of Jacob forever, and of his kingdom there will be no end."
— Luke 1:28-33

This is a good presentation for a small group or for very young children. Take slides of your children in costume on location. *(For locations use a farm or the humane society or any natural type setting for traditional Advent scenes. The background is not as important as the children are.)* When presenting the program, the older children can read the parts *(a large Bible would be nice)* accompanied by a Children's or Youth Choir as the slides are being shown.

One thing that makes this presentation special is that the children can watch themselves as they participate in the program. Then, too, you have a beautiful record to keep. Many parents will want prints of the slides in which their children appear.

Charactors

Narrator	Child Three
Child One	Child Four
Angel	Choir
Child Two	

(Setting: Slide projector, large screen or white wall, speakers' stand with large Bible, a raised area near the front of room for your choir [Children in choir should stand where they can see slides].)

Narrator: *"The angel Gabriel was sent by God to a town in Galilee called Nazareth, to a virgin engaged to a man whose name was Joseph, of the house of David. The virgin's name was Mary"* (Luke 26-30).

Child One: The Angel came to her and said:

Angel: *"Greetings, favored one! The Lord is with you. Do not be afraid, Mary, for you have found favor with God. And now, you will conceive in your womb and bear a son, and you will name him Jesus. He will be great, and will be called the Son of the Most High, and the Lord God will give to him the throne of his ancestor David. He will reign over the house of Jacob forever, and of his kingdom there will be no end"* (Luke 1:28-33).

Choir: "The King Of Glory Comes"

Narrator: Emperor Augustus ordered that everyone was to go to the town of his forefathers to register himself for the taxes.

Child Two: Joseph, being a descendent of King David, went to Bethlehem. Joseph went and took Mary, his betrothed, with him.

Choir: "Joseph Came A'walking"

Picture: Mary riding donkey with Joseph leading. *(You could use a real donkey or horse or just have Mary and Joseph walking on a country road)*

Child Three: When they reached Bethlehem there was no room for them to stay in the Inn, so they had to stay in a stable.

Narrator: While they were in Bethlehem the time came for her to have her baby, and she gave birth to her first son, wrapped him in swaddling cloths and laid him in a manger.

Choir: "Away In A Manger"

Picture: Mary and Joseph in a stable. *(It would be nice if there were a few animals, real or stuffed toys, in view.)* Mary is holding a baby *(real if possible)*.

Narrator: Out in the fields, some shepherds were caring for their flocks.

Choir: "The First Noel"

Picture: Shepherds on a hillside or grassy area with a few sheep around them. *(Stuffed toys or cardboard animals will do)*

Narrator: An Angel of the Lord appeared to them and the glory of the Lord shone all about them. And the Shepherds were terribly afraid.

Child One: But the Angel said to them:

Angel: Don't be afraid, I have come with good news which will bring great joy to all people. This very day in David's town, your Savior, Christ, the Lord is born. And this is what will prove it to you. You will find a baby wrapped in cloths and lying in a manger.

Narrator: Suddenly, there was a great number of Heaven's angels singing praises to God.

Choir: "Angels We Have Heard On High"

Picture: Angels singing in different poses. *(An effective way to take this picture is to lay yourself on the ground with the camera and have the angels, in costume, gather around in a circle over top of you and look down at the camera. This gives the impression of angels looking down from heaven)*

Child Two: Let us go to Bethlehem and see this thing that the Angels have told us.

Narrator: *"So they went with haste, and found Mary and Joseph, and the child lying in the manger"* (Luke 2:16).

54

Choir: "Silent Night, Holy Night"

Picture: Stable with Nativity Scene including Shepherds.

Narrator: *"When they saw this, they made known what had been told them about his child, and all who heard it were amazed at what the shepherds told them. But, Mary treasured all these words and pondered them in her heart. The shepherds returned, glorifying and praising God for all they had heard and seen, as it had been told them"* (Luke 2:17-20).

Choir: "On A Cold And Lonely Night"

Picture: The night sky with a bright star ... if possible, a small town included. *(Try taking a picture of a Christmas card, or perhaps a night picture of your own town)*

Narrator: Far in the East some men who studied the stars noticed a special star in the sky. They set out to follow it for they believed that a star foretold a special event. When they reached Jerusalem they approached King Herod.

Picture: Three Kings dressed in fine robes walking along the road ... or the Kings approaching King Herod on his throne.

Child Three: Where is the baby born to be King of the Jews? We have seen his star when it came up in the East and have come to worship him.

Narrator: King Herod was very upset, as was everyone in Jerusalem. He called together all the Chief Priests and Teachers of the Law and asked them:

Child One: Just where will the Messiah be born?

Child Two: In the town of Bethlehem in Judea.

Narrator: Herod sent them to Bethlehem and said:

Child Four: Go, and make a careful search for the child and when you find him let me know so that I, too, may go and worship him.

Narrator: When they came to Bethlehem they found the child with his mother Mary, and they knelt down and worshiped him. They brought out their gifts of gold, frankincense, and myrrh and presented them to him.

Picture: Kings offering gifts at the manger.

Choir and Congregation: "Joy To The World"

The End

The children of

present

You Are There

by Doris Wells Miller

"When they saw this, they made known what had been told them about his child, and all who heard it were amazed at what the shepherds told them. But, Mary treasured all these words and pondered them in her heart. The shepherds returned, glorifying and praising God for all they had heard and seen, as it had been told them" (Luke 2:17-20).

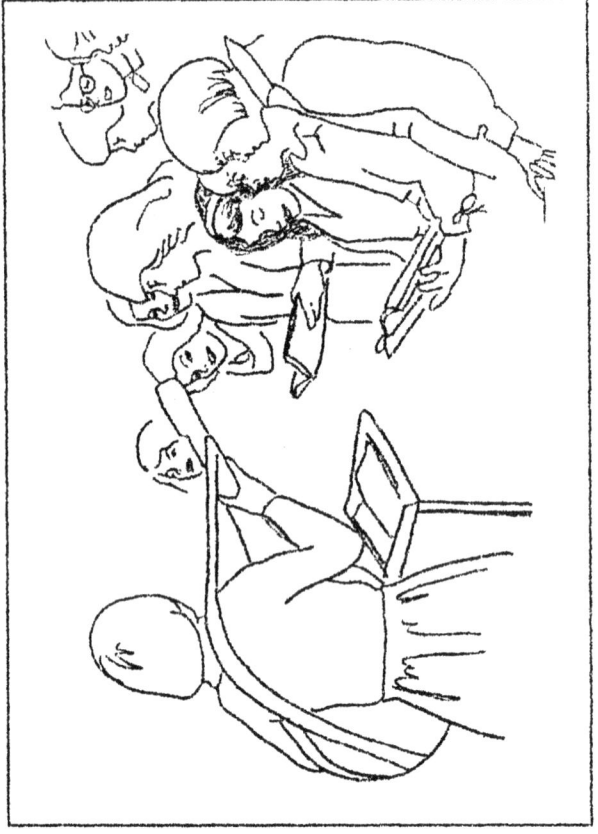

You Are There

"Greetings, favored one! The Lord is with you. Do not be afraid, Mary, for you have found favor with God. And now, you will conceive in your womb and bear a son, and you will name him Jesus. He will be great, and will be called the Son of the Most High, and the Lord God will give to him the throne of his ancestor David. He will reign over the house of Jacob forever, and of his kingdom there will be no end" (Luke 1:28-33).

www.ingramcontent.com/pod-product-compliance
Lightning Source LLC
Chambersburg PA
CBHW050357100426
42739CB00015BB/3425